Sally Ride:
Trailblazer in Space

Mc
Graw
Hill
SRA

Columbus, OH

SRAonline.com

 SRA

Send all inquiries to this address:
SRA/McGraw-Hill
4400 Easton Commons
Columbus, OH 43219

ISBN: 978-0-07-608760-0
MHID: 0-07-608760-3

1 2 3 4 5 6 7 8 9 NOR 13 12 11 10 09 08 07

The *McGraw-Hill* Companies

The visitor center at Johnson Space Center

Welcome to Johnson Space Center. This is one of the toughest schools in the world. Like students everywhere, students here listen to their teachers. They read their textbooks. Unlike other students, though, students here have to learn to fly a jet. They learn how to get out if that jet is in trouble. They learn how to move when there is no gravity holding them down. They learn how to use and repair very complex machines. These students are training to be astronauts.

Ride was born in California in 1951. One of her hobbies was tennis. She worked hard at it. She was one of the top young tennis players in the United States. For a while she focused on making a career as a tennis player.

This changed when Ride went to college. She took a lot of English classes. She thought she would become an English teacher. But she was really good at science too.

Ride studied a branch of science called physics. Physics is the study of different forces, like gravity and friction, and processes that change these forces. Ride found science very interesting. She loved studying physics.

When she finished college, Ride was ready for a new adventure. Science was very important to her. She wanted to do something special with all of her science knowledge. What could be better than flying on a space mission?

Her success at sports and her good education had given Ride confidence. She applied to the astronaut training program. She knew she could use her knowledge and skills to help on a space mission. She also knew she was smart enough to learn everything the program would teach her about space. Few women had tried to become astronauts. Ride wanted to see that change. Only two other women had ever gone into space. They were Russian.

To become a mission specialist, Ride had to learn many new things. She had to keep track of all of the fuel, water, and food used on a mission. She needed to know how every part of a space shuttle worked. She had to learn to do the types of tests she would run in space. Ride knew that she might even have to walk in space. She studied very hard at the space center!

Ride did important work on these missions. On the *Challenger* she helped put satellites into orbit. She tested a robotic arm that was used to grab and work on space objects. She ran tests that would help on future space flights. She took pictures of Earth that would help with research.

Ride was ready to go back into space. However, in 1986 a problem caused the *Challenger* to explode just after launching. Her mission was called off. NASA had to build a new, safer space shuttle.

Ride helped study what caused the *Challenger* accident. She continued to help NASA make plans for future space missions. Then she left NASA to become a teacher. She taught physics in California. Ride also ran the California Space Institute.

She had inspired many people when she was an astronaut. She also inspired them as a teacher and public speaker. Ride used her experience as an astronaut to advance people's interest in science.

Ride talking to Ground Control

Ride speaking for the Advancement of Girls in Math and Science (May 2006)

As the first U.S. woman in space, Ride set an example for girls. She had always been one of only a few women in her field. She knew that sometimes girls were discouraged from becoming scientists. Ride thought it was important to change that. She started working on ways to get all young people, but especially girls, excited about math and science. She wrote books about space for children. She wanted everyone to know about the importance of science.

Ride was a pioneer. She became an astronaut at a time when many people weren't sure women should be astronauts. She proved that women could succeed in space and science in general.

Ride's boldness paved the way for other women to join the space program. She still works to get young people excited about science and technology. Ride shows people everywhere how to aim high and reach for the stars.

Vocabulary

application (ap´ li kā´ shən) (page 4) *n.* A request, especially for a job.

focused (fō´ kəst) (page 6) *v.* Past tense of **focus:** To direct attention to someone or something.

processes (prä´ se səz´) (page 6) *n.* Plural form of **process:** A series of actions performed in making or doing something.

confidence (kon´ fə dəns) (page 9) *n.* Faith in oneself.

sensations (sen sā´ shənz) (page 10) *n.* Plural form of **sensation:** A feeling.

advance (ad vans´) (page 12) *v.* To help the progress or growth of; further.

Comprehension Focus: Adjust Reading Speed

1. Ride had to do a lot of studying and reading to learn about space. When you read something that is very difficult or detailed, what is one thing you can do to make sure you understand what you are reading?

2. Which sections of the text did you find confusing? How did you adjust your reading speed to help you understand the selection?